First World War
and Army of Occupation
War Diary
France, Belgium and Germany

28 DIVISION
Divisional Troops
Royal Army Service Corps
Divisional Train (170, 171, 172, 173 Companies A.S.C.)
15 January 1915 - 17 November 1915

WO95/2272/9

The Naval & Military Press Ltd
www.nmarchive.com
Published in association with The National Archives

Published by

The Naval & Military Press Ltd

Unit 10 Ridgewood Industrial Park,

Uckfield, East Sussex,

TN22 5QE England

Tel: +44 (0) 1825 749494

www.naval-military-press.com

www.nmarchive.com

This diary has been reprinted in facsimile from the original. Any imperfections are inevitably reproduced and the quality may fall short of modern type and cartographic standards.

© **Crown Copyright**
Images reproduced by permission of The National Archives, London, England, 2015.

Contents

Document type	Place/Title	Date From	Date To
Heading	WO95/2272/9		
Heading	28th Division Divl Troops 28th Divl Train A.S.C. Jan-Nov 1915 (170 To 173 Coys ASC) 170 Coy Transferred To 33 Div Train 171 Coy Transferred To 33 Div Train 173 Coy Transferred To 33 Div Train 172 Coy Transferred To 2 Div Train		
Heading	28th Divisional Train Vol I 15-30.1.15		
War Diary	Winchester	15/01/1915	15/01/1915
War Diary	Hursley Camp Winchester	15/01/1915	15/01/1915
War Diary	Southampton	15/01/1915	15/01/1915
War Diary	Winchester	16/01/1915	16/01/1915
War Diary	Havre	16/01/1915	16/01/1915
War Diary	Southampton	16/01/1915	16/01/1915
War Diary	Havre	17/01/1915	17/01/1915
War Diary	Winchester	17/01/1915	17/01/1915
War Diary	Southampton	17/01/1915	17/01/1915
War Diary	Hazebruck	18/01/1915	18/01/1915
War Diary	Havre	18/01/1915	18/01/1915
War Diary	Borre	18/01/1915	18/01/1915
War Diary	Outtersteene	18/01/1915	18/01/1915
War Diary	Havre	19/01/1915	20/01/1915
War Diary	Hazebruck	21/01/1915	21/01/1915
War Diary	Caestre	21/01/1915	21/01/1915
War Diary	Hazebruck	21/01/1915	30/01/1915
Heading	28th Divn Train Vol II 30.1-28.2.15		
War Diary		30/01/1915	28/02/1915
Heading	28th Divisional Train Vol III 1-31.3.15		
War Diary		01/03/1915	31/03/1915
Heading	28th Divl Train Vol IV 1-30.4.15		
War Diary		01/04/1915	30/04/1915
Heading	28th Division 28th Divisional Trains Vol V 121/5574		
War Diary		01/05/1915	31/05/1915
Heading	28 Division 28th Divl Trains Vol VI 2-30.6.15 121/5872		
War Diary		02/06/1915	30/06/1915
Heading	28th Division 28th Divisional Trains Vol VII July 15 121/6292		
War Diary		01/07/1915	31/07/1915
Heading	28th Division 28th Divl Trains Vol VIII August 15 121/6857		
War Diary		01/08/1915	30/08/1915
Heading	28th Division 28th Divl Trains Vol IX Sept 15 121/7100		
War Diary		01/09/1915	30/09/1915
Heading	28th Division 28th Divl Trains Oct 1915 Vol X 121/7519		
War Diary		01/10/1915	31/10/1915
Heading	28th Divn Trains Nov Vol XI 121/7779		
War Diary		01/11/1915	17/11/1915

wo 95/22229(a)

wo 95/22229(a)

28TH DIVISION
DIVL TROOPS

28TH DIVL TRAIN A.S.C.

JAN - NOV 1915

(170 TO 173 COYS ASC)

170 COY TRANSFERRED TO 33 DIV TRAIN
171 " " " " " "
173 " " " " " "
172 " " " 2 " "

121/4/95

28th Divisional Train.

Vol I.

15-30.1.15

Army Form C. 2118.

WAR DIARY
or
INTELLIGENCE SUMMARY.
(Erase heading not required.)

Instructions regarding War Diaries and Intelligence Summaries are contained in F.S. Regs., Part II and the Staff Manual respectively. Title pages will be prepared in manuscript.

28¹ Divl Train

Hour, Date, Place	Summary of Events and Information	Remarks and references to Appendices
9.0 am 15/1/15 Manchester	No 2 Coy 28 Divl Train left Manchester en route for Southampton.	
10.40 am 15/1/15 Headly Downs Manchester	Head Qrs + Head Qrs company left Headly en route for Southampton.	
1.40 pm 15/1/15 Southampton	No 2 Coy arrived at Southampton Docks + proceeded to embark on SS City of Edinburgh – 9 horses exchanged with remount department	
2.40 pm 15/1/15 Southampton	Head Qrs + Head Qrs company arrived at Southampton Docks + proceeded to embark on SS City of Oxford Hall – 3 horses exchanged with remount department	
5.30 pm 15/1/15	SS City of Edinburgh sailed	
6.0 pm 15/1/15	SS City of Oxford Hall sailed	

Army Form C. 2118.

2 S 1 Grof [?]

WAR DIARY
or
INTELLIGENCE SUMMARY.
(Erase heading not required.)

Instructions regarding War Diaries and Intelligence Summaries are contained in F. S. Regs., Part II. and the Staff Manual respectively. Title pages will be prepared in manuscript.

Hour, Date, Place	Summary of Events and Information	Remarks and references to Appendices
10 am 16/1/15 Manchester	1/3 Coy left Manchester en route for Southampton.	
12 noon 16/1/15 Havre	No 2 Coy billeted in Hangar Docks proceeded to Dieumstead. The horses were stabled at the HANGAR AUX COTONS for the night, the wagons were packed on the Wharf & the personnel housed in a shed on the docks. French Interpreter M Picard joined the company.	
3.30 pm 16/1/15 Southampton	No 3 Coy arrived at Southampton Docks & embarked on SS City of Chester	
16/1/15	Hd of 2s company at sea off Havre	
2 am 17/1/15 Havre	Hd of 2s company in SS Trafford Hall berthed in Havre Docks at 2 am, started to disembark at 4.30 am (delay caused by the non arrival of the stevedores) finished disemb- arking at 8.30 am & immediately marched to Havre Goods	

WAR DIARY
or
INTELLIGENCE SUMMARY.

(Erase heading not required.)

Army Form C. 2118.

3

Hour, Date, Place	Summary of Events and Information	Remarks and references to Appendices
ROUEN		
10.19 am 17/1/15 Manchester	Station where the Company was entrained together with No 2 company, two platoons of the HQ & 1 + one sect. of No 1 company, the whole under the command of	
10.0 pm 17/1/15	Major Stough RSE. Train left Heaton	
2.0 pm 17/1/15 Southampton	Left Manchester en route for Southampton. No 1 coy arrived at Southampton + embarked on "SS Archimedes". Sub Lieuten exchanged with Lieutenant Bryant. Sergt F. Macdonald erected his pont under a rope.	
17/1/15	whilst at Sea. 2nd Lieut Jackson No 2 coy fell behind at Stearn with	
9.30 am 18/1/15 HAZEBROUCK	Train containing Head Qr company + No 2 company arrived at Hazebrouck. Disentrained + proceeded to march to Pont Felleting Bries. The former to BORRE + the latter	

WAR DIARY
or
INTELLIGENCE SUMMARY.
(Erase heading not required.)

Army Form C. 2118.

Instructions regarding War Diaries and Intelligence Summaries are contained in F.S. Regs., Part II. and the Staff Manual respectively. Title pages will be prepared in manuscript.

Hour, Date, Place		Summary of Events and Information	Remarks and references to Appendices
11 am 18/1/15	HAVRE	to OUTTERSTEENE	
		No 3 Coy disembarked at Havre & proceeded to Le Havre camp, also No 4 company, which had one casualty viz Pte Bowden H.E. who fell down one the steps of the ship & broke some ribs, admitted to H.	
18/1/15	BORRE	Head Dr company in billets	
"	OUTTERSTEENE	No 2 company killed	
19/1/15	HAVRE	Nos 3 & 4 companies in Le Havre camp	
5.30 pm 29/1/15	HAVRE	Remainder as for previous day	
9.20 pm " "	"	No 3 company entrained at Havre Goods Station	
9.0 am 20/1/15	"	" " " Left Havre in route for Hazebrouck	
		" " " entrained at Havre Station. Left one hour behind at Base H.T. depot	
		Remainder as for previous day	

WAR DIARY
or
INTELLIGENCE SUMMARY.

(Erase heading not required.)

Army Form C. 2118.

5

Hour, Date, Place	Summary of Events and Information	Remarks and references to Appendices
10.30am 20/1/15 HAZEBROUCK	No 4 company arrived & disembarked. March to	
3.30pm CAESTRE	CAESTRE where the company goes into billets in a farm NE of the railway Station.	
8pm 20/1/15 HAZEBROUCK	No 3 company arrived & disembarked & go into billets in the town	
9.30 am 21/1/15	No 3 company march out of HAZEBROUCK & march to STRAZEELE where it goes into billets.	
22/1/15	Remainder as on previous day	
	Head Quarters & No 1 company in billets at BORRE	
23/1/15	" " " " OOTTERSTEENE	
24/1/15	No 2 " " " "	
	" 3 " " " " STRAZEELE	
25/1/15	" 4 " " " " CAESTRE	25/1/15 No 2 Coy one HD horse admitted to hosp out Section suspected Scabies

Army Form C. 2118.

WAR DIARY
or
INTELLIGENCE SUMMARY.
(Erase heading not required.)

Instructions regarding War Diaries and Intelligence Summaries are contained in F.S. Regs., Part II and the Staff Manual respectively. Title pages will be prepared in manuscript.

Hour, Date, Place	Summary of Events and Information	Remarks and references to Appendices
26/1/15	HdQrs 1n company in billets at BORRE	26/1/15 No 2 coy one NCO horse died of Pneumonia
27/1/15	No 2 " " " " OUTTERSTEENE	27/1/16 No 4 coy one NCO horse died of Pneumonia
	" 3 " " " " STRAZEELE	
	" 4 " " " " CAESTRE	
28/1/15	Inspection of harness by OC in C.	
	Billets as above	
29/1/15	12 m Coonly of London Regt joins the division & is attached to 83rd brigade.	
30/1/15	Belgian interpreters attached for duty as under	Horse admitted to Vet Hosp returned to duty No 2 coy. 30/1/15
29/1/15	Head Dr Coy Mons. Bergman Jules	
	Head Dr Company Mons. Huyghoudt Camille	
	No 2 " " Donckaert Charles	
	" 3 " " van Hilst Joseph	
	" 4 " " Semmett Camille	

121/4506

25th Div¹ Trans

Vol II   30.1 — 28.2.15

Army Form C. 2118.

WAR DIARY
or
INTELLIGENCE SUMMARY.
(Erase heading not required.)

28 Divl Train

Hour, Date, Place	Summary of Events and Information	Remarks and references to Appendices
30/1/15	Hd Qrs company in billets at BORRE	No 2 drawn 3 HD Horses from Remounts 31/1/15
1/2/15	No 2 " " " " OOSTERSTEENE	4427 Pry 1 HD horse destroyed
	" 3 " " " " STRAZEELE	Pg Yo 1/2/15
	" 4 " " " " CAESTRE	No 4 Coy drawn 1 officers charger
2/2/15	Divisional Train left its billeting area on its march to BAILLEUL	& 2 HD horses from Remounts 3/4/15
	thro N. Starting point Notre Dame Church 9am, route BAILLEUL	7/14091 25 the Battalion & 2 Company
3/2/15	LOCRE-RENINGHELST to area SW of VLAMATINGHE. In	admitted to 3/2/15
4/2/15	billets by 1230 pm	No 2 Coy 1 RSD & 1 man admitted
5/2/15	Train remained in billets	to H 5/2/15
6/2/15	Head Quarter of Train moved into POPERINGHE alongside	7/14/037600 Pam S.F. Serjeant H
	Divisional Headquarters.	7/14/027560 St Certificant S.E
7/2/15	Advanced transport depot established at VLAMERTINGHE to deal	
	with urgent transport work (1 officer & 6 wagons, companies to	
	perform these duties in rotation)	

Army Form C. 2118.

WAR DIARY
or
INTELLIGENCE SUMMARY.
(Erase heading not required.)

2 8 Divl Train

Instructions regarding War Diaries and Intelligence Summaries are contained in F. S. Regs., Part II and the Staff Manual respectively. Title pages will be prepared in manuscript.

Hour, Date, Place	Summary of Events and Information	Remarks and references to Appendices
8/2/15	No name Pellett	T/32767 Pt Angle S admitted HP 6.2.15. + T/4/037363 Pt Fitzgerald admitted HP 10/2/15. T/037549 Pt Beevers admitted HP 9/2/15.
9/2/15		
10/2/15	9 G.S. wagons (7 from 1 Divl A.C. + 2 from 2 Divl A.C.) report for work with Belgian artillery. Attached to Head Qrs company.	
11/2/15		3 horses (1 O + 2 HD) admitted V.O. 9/2/15. 1 HD died 10/2/15 his ek say.
12/2/15	15 G.S. wagons for hay arrive from advanced H.Q depôt (11 for escort Brigade company + the remainder for Headquarter company) Capt Reynolds sent to Belgian artillery to help them in their supply work	1 HD has 3 coy died (Strangles) 13/2/15
13/2/15		T/4/037726 Pt Hollingworth L admitted HP 12/2/15.
14/2/15		T/4/037724 Pt J Hinchley a admitted HP 16/2/15
15/2/15		T/2SR/0991 Pt Carter W admitted HP 16/2/15
16/2/15		T/2SR/0999 S Legg A admitted HP 7/2/15. T/4/037529 Sgt Hill Re T/2SR 0484
17/2/15	Transport depôt of 12 wagons under Lieut Pawlence established at POPERINGHE for local transport work. Advanced part at VLAMERTINGHE washed out... Sergt Seuil squad goes reports for duty & is posted to Head Quarter company.	Pt Davies D admitted HP 7/2/15. T/4/037549 Pt Beacon WR admit HP 14/2/15. T/2SR/01491 Pt Walker W admitted HP 18/2/15
18/2/15		

WAR DIARY or INTELLIGENCE SUMMARY

Army Form C. 2118.

(Erase heading not required.)

28 Divl Train

Instructions regarding War Diaries and Intelligence Summaries are contained in F.S. Regs., Part II. and the Staff Manual respectively. Title pages will be prepared in manuscript.

Hour, Date, Place	Summary of Events and Information	Remarks and references to Appendices
19/2/15	No recent killed. No 3 company horses converted to 4 x 11 h.p. 84 rifle + 2 rifles & 8 H.D. No 2 company heavy 8 horses (2 h.p. 82" rifle) for the company. No 2 company has to fill to a form G.11.a. – 9 x 4 h.p. rifle as company moves from to [?] to cook to rest. Wagons are exchanged between 95 & which gives had to cook to rest. Wagons are exchanged between the 9 x 4 h.p. No. 3 company 9/85 rifles completed. — 2/Lieut Bowen admitted to No 3 clearing H...	T/4/037084 Dr Blake reported from HP 19/2/15 T/w-335 Dr Ironsides resignin 25 day. ASC 19/2/15 S/23586 Dr Brown to + T/3331 Dr Marshall from Hosp. 5th Dvl Mon 21/2/15 also T/SR/1330 Dr Harding to P – T/28691 Dr Moff W + T/37485 Dr Halliday PR from 6 Dvl Amn 21/2/15.
20/2/15	Exchange between 9 + 85 rifles completed. — 2/Lieut Bowen admitted to No 3 clearing H — 6 years wagons's horses transferred from No 2 sup to No 2 sup for duty as hay wagons	2 H.D. horses per sup. sup. with by V.D., 3 H.D. + 2 Light Draught sent to Vet H. 21/2/15
21/2/15		2 H.D. mares on foot and to Railhead en route to Base — 1 H.D. horse to Vet H — No 2 company 22/2/15
22/2/15		1 H.D. lost by No 2 coy
23/2/15	T / Dr Bruce No 3 coy tried by F.G.C.M for drunkenness — No. 3 company	T/9443 4/cpl Capron L. admitted HP 19/2/15. T/14/037331 Dr Holmes sick admitted HP 24/2/15. T/SR/01799 Dr Blake H admitted HP 21/2/15
24/2/15	T / marches to BAILLEUL	
25/2/15		
26/2/15		
27/2/15	2/Lieut Bowen rejoins for duty from HP	
28/2/15		

8th Divisional Train

Vol III 1 — 31.3.15

Army Form C. 2118.

WAR DIARY
or
INTELLIGENCE SUMMARY.
(Erase heading not required.)

28 Divl Train

10

Hour, Date, Place	Summary of Events and Information	Remarks and references to Appendices
2pft 1/3/15	Train still on same billets	1 HD horse destroyed (incurable) 28/2/15. M+S Coy. 1 L.D. horse send to 2nd Vet Sec. HS Coy 3.3.15.
	S/Sgt E DAC RFA attached to 28 Divl Train tried by F.G.C.M. for absence from evening roll call 14/2/15 until apprehended by M.P. at 7.20 pm on 17/2/15	1 HD mare dead 2/3/15. 1 LD horse shot by VO 3/3/15. 1 LD horse received from dead det on 5/3/15. Relf of M+S Coy
2/3/15	Major Blough admitted to No 10 Stationary H dangerously ill suffering from spotted fever	1 HD horse to Rest Vet Sec 4/3/15 - as on 1 HD horse shot by VO 5/3/15 7/2/58/pigeon S/Sgts & admitted H 28/2/15
3/3/15	Promulgation of proceedings in the case of S/Sgt -	
4/3/15	RFA drivers sent to the Belgian batteries retained to make warning from RA 8 now replaced by OSC drivers - the 3 company having returned from 3 Div. takes over the transport work of the 15 Inf Bde. whole H2 company that of the 13 Inf Bde. but the supply details continue to feed their respective brigades	2 HD horses died Not 2n Coy 6/3/15 1 HD horse shot horse Coy 9/3/15 Not 2n Coy - 2 R horses received from Res at 8/2/15. 1 HD horse died at Not Coy 12/3/15 7/1/158/597 S/Tailor admitted H 9/3/15
5/3/15	H2 2S company receives 9 HD horses from Ing Coll RFA.	7/40/637/44 Cpl Light 11/3/15 7/255/01788 D Sanitary 9/3/15
6/3/15		
7/3/15	He IX draws 9 HD horses from Ing battery, 2 and 16 He 2n Coy	
8/3/15		
9/3/15		
10/3/15		
11/3/15	S/sgt of M coon from tease, 2 for Med 2n coy, 3 for the remaining companies	
12/3/15	Major Blough died at for Cross H. - 6 remounts received from Sunny Germany	

M 148 D Lazy at For 2 coy 3 for 3 coy 2 for 4 coy

Forms/C. 2118/10.

WAR DIARY
or
INTELLIGENCE SUMMARY.

(Erase heading not required.) 28 3rd Fm

Army Form C. 2118.

Hour, Date, Place	Summary of Events and Information	Remarks and references to Appendices
13/3/15	In camp Killubo	2 H.D horse shoe #24 by 13/3/15 1 HD horse shoe 2 by 14/3/15
14/3/15		
15/3/15	ADMS inspected Killubo	
16/3/15	Promulgation of proceedings of 14.4.m on the rear Sgt Tuck 2 coy relieved to the ranks	
17/3/15	Inspection of horses by DDQR	
18/3/15	Sgt Major Storms reduced to the ranks	
19/3/15	Staff leaves for the Base. 2, Os. 3 Rs + 3 H Ds received from Remounts	Sgt Brompton. P/Sgt Hoole. Pte While Pte Hazlet. Pte Smith. SB Powell. Pte from Pte Staff. QSM Slaney Sgt Matthew
20/3/15	Lieut Glenbergs moved to new billeting area about 2 miles E of rest. and R.S Wagon Sew. 1s Section 17 Manning Co RE from HO 2nd Cav Brigade + 5th Cav Brigade	Corpl Nicholls. SOMS Halet. Pte Rayment SOMS Peveke. Pte Taylor. Sgt Watch. L/Cpl Mullie.
21/3/15		1 ND horse shoe N°2 a. Cy 21/3/15
22/3/15	Sent A.D Ambulance Ambulance to H.Q and cleared to new	1 ND horse shoe 3 cy 23/3/15
23/3/15	FS Convoy exchanged 4 F.S Wagons for 4 civilian Wagons lent to 10th R Cav Reg.	114/03/362 Watson Admitted Ah 24/3/15
24/3/15		14/03/571 Atkinson A2 adm Pb 24/3/15
25/3/15	One Supplies R.S Wagon loaned one to 9th Sedan Reg. by HQ 2nd Cav	T258/0/95 Mi Diks J. Comp Al 24/3/15
26/3/15	Captain Norman admitted to 2nd London Field ambulance	54/044/74 Pte Kerr W. Lost HC + H 25/3/15
27/3/15	The officers of each section who is the whole of Sunday to go in to heave mare from. the whole of fitter being equipped as 3 lys were … [illegible]	14/00/1766 Smith admitted HP 22/3/15

CA

WAR DIARY
or
INTELLIGENCE SUMMARY.
(Erase heading not required.) 28 Sial Train

Army Form C. 2118.

12

Instructions regarding War Diaries and Intelligence Summaries are contained in F. S. Regs., Part II. and the Staff Manual respectively. Title pages will be prepared in manuscript.

Hour, Date, Place	Summary of Events and Information	Remarks and references to Appendices
28/3/15	3rd Coy drill. H.Q. 2nd Co drove 5 H.D. horses 3 Co 6 A.D. horses 4 Co 6 H.T. horses	1 &D. horses sent to W.O.S. cavalry stables 30.3.15 1 HD horse exchanged 30.3.15 31.3.15 1 HD aw. cavalry 3 Coy 31.3.15
29/3/15		
30/3/15	2.3. and 4 Civilian Surgeons wagons returned to Ordnance. H.Q. Co. Lewis S.S. wagon returned to Ordnance. 5 Ordnance & W.O.S. Coy. Captain would supplement with mules.	
31/3/15	1 S.S. wagon returned to Ordnance & W.O.S. Coy.	

General remarks:—Quarters hard. G.S. wagons need overhaul for Embarkation. Transport by R.

2. Emergency turnries– fair.

3. Limber wagon "connections" require attention. They are not strong enough.

4. Spare wheels issued were, in many cases, found to be useless and did not fit. This has now been put right.

5. Guns apparently no experiments in keeping loads with Train wagons to steady.

(a) R.A. Units and, when found, and by no means well looked after – They appear to be no one's child – with the exception of the "Supply Column" Divisional Troops all other transport should be "regimental" the remaining wagons being for baggage and stores should remain with the batteries, available for movement at any time.

C.I.

25ter Dio d'Irani

Vol IV 1 — 30.4.15

Army Form C. 2118.

WAR DIARY
or
INTELLIGENCE SUMMARY.
(Erase heading not required.)

2ⁿᵈ Divisional Train

13

Instructions regarding War Diaries and Intelligence Summaries are contained in F.S. Regs., Part II. and the Staff Manual respectively. Title pages will be prepared in manuscript.

Hour, Date, Place	Summary of Events and Information	Remarks and references to Appendices
1/4/15	Sir Ernest Willetts Capt. Reynolds takes over command of HQ 2 Coys	1 HD horse and L. Mot Var Sec of No 2 Coy 1.4.15
2/4/15	9 wagons sent by No 3 Co to No 4 Co to assist in move of 9th Regt	2 HD horse sec L. Mot var sec of No 2 Co 1.4.15
3/4/15	HQ 2 Co to receive 2 HD horse from 1st Mot Var Sec. The 9 wagons leave No 3 Co to No 4 Co to return Exchange of wagons effected by No 4 Co	1 HD horse attached to No. HQ 2 Co 3.4.15 T/4/027665 C 2 M.S. Alexander W.E. T/4/02767 Sergt. Swainbanks T/4/02/390 cpl. Amos left to HT's attached 5.4.15
4/4/15	1 NCO & 5 gun fan return to HQ 2 Co 5 from 75th Bdy RFA Train Casualties at No 4 Co	T/4/027700 to Serving to T/4/50/262 to Serving T/4/027/51 to Serving to T/4/02/7743 T/4 028 to T/4/027881 Recruit A T/3/027881 to Commant
5/4/15	5 horses transferred from No 3 Co & 2 to No 2 Co & L No 2 Co DK No 2 G. No 2 Co receives 2 H.B. horses from Mot Var Sec. 3 NCOs leave for H.T. Dilldetail	Posted to L. No 2 Co 5.4.15 1 LD horse att. to No 4 Co 6.4.15
6/4/15	SQMS Clany 2/10/732 transferred to Sgt staff 2nd Divn. 2 W.Os arrive from and T/12/50 SSM Hengler + attached L. No 2 Co L T/13855 Standby R.H. + posted L. No 2 Co No 2 Co horse to WESTOUTRE w/wagons 83rd Divn	
7/4/15 8/4/15	Companies move to new billets NE of old Companies completed wagon loading ammunition to wagon + in return to 75th B & y R.F.A.	

Army Form C. 2118.

WAR DIARY
or
INTELLIGENCE SUMMARY.
(Erase heading not required.)

28th Divisional Train

14

Hour, Date, Place	Summary of Events and Information	Remarks and references to Appendices
9/4/15	On arrival No 2 Coy detrained from Westoutre and occupied billets and commenced to establish in Locretere.	As above C.R. admit WHP 11.4.15 from No 2 C. IHD horse sent C. Mob vet sec. 2 No 2 Coy 12.4.15
10/4/15	A Coy 6 mens killed horses killed N.E. of LAMERTINGHE and No 3 Co commenced HD horses arrives in billets at No 3 Co.	
11/4/15	Supply Personnel again in Coys. 2 wagons + ammunition + supply ... 1 Sgt + 2 Dvrs + 2 horses + 1 GS wagon 5.11 & N...	
12/4/15	Supply Section of Train Reserve Troops concentrated T/13855 S.S.N. Tomlin R.H. admitted HP drowned. 21 SD horse + 2 mules drawn No 3 Co for Brigade Troops Coys + B ... ordered on exercise etc ...	
13/4/15	No 3 Co on exchange baggage wagons all 4 by Staff train.	
14/4/15	T. Smith 5227 arrived on attached Ly No 2 Coy + 28 C. aviation for from No 2 Co to No 3 Co. Engy 8 men from SENC Tpt to No 2 Co. 3 L. No 4 Co. No 2 Co received 10 SD horses for Brigade Troops from No 3 Co + drew 4 HD horses + 15 D horses for Coys No 4 L drew + 1 officer charger.	T/4037698 C 2 MS felt/rose C 2 MS 11 T/4037599 Sergt Reed 35 T/4037 596 2/Cpl Semyk C T/4037 181 Sept ... A transferred 4 HT Sept attached K WWL 1 3 7 Statmen 23 Dvols 2 hylas 2 110 local By Dolds 5 Sh... Dvds 5 Sechen + Walt Smith O/Servi... CA
15/4/15	Brig ? Reserve for England. Horses for Brigade Troops drawn by No 2 + B Co No 2 Co drew 2 IID horses	

Forms/C. 2118/10.

WAR DIARY
or
INTELLIGENCE SUMMARY.
(Erase heading not required.) 2(?) Sial Train

Army Form C. 2118.

Hour, Date, Place	Summary of Events and Information	Remarks and references to Appendices
16/4/15	Sir Comm Militte Capt Skelton leaves for England on 4 days leave. Comm returns to HP and is from HM is travelling to Bn	T/SR/031/54 as amended J.S. HP 16.4.15
17/4/15		T/ISR/0125 4 Br Buckley 9 Transferor & taught employment wounded 17.4.15. 1 change ordered by V.O. HP 2vs17/4/15 T/33548 to Sceers as admitted HP 18.4.15
18/4/15	2/Lt AP Brown transferred to advanced HT Depot	
19/4/15	3 HD horses cast by N° 2 ro confry 5 85th Bgde H° 2 rs by flor casualties	
20/4/15	N° 4 Coy after unloaded G's days rations 6 motor in lieu of horses for 85th Bgde H° 2 ro	1 HD horse destroyed V.O. H° 2vs G 20.4.15
21/4/15	Train H° 2 rs removes from POPERINGHE to VLAMERTINGHE	
22/4/15	On account of German attack on Ypres Salient it became necessary to move H° 2rs to a point 1½ miles west of VLAMERTINGHE and orders were issued for the train to be in readiness to move	1 HD horse destroyed V.O. H° 2vs G 22.4.15
23/4/15	N°s 2 & 4 Cos removed to a point 1½ miles west of the old billets	TR 499 Sr Parter Reserve G wounded & admitted HP 23.4.15
		CA

WAR DIARY
or
INTELLIGENCE SUMMARY.
(Erase heading not required.)   28th East Train

Army Form C. 2118.

16

Instructions regarding War Diaries and Intelligence Summaries are contained in F.S. Regs., Part II. and the Staff Manual respectively. Title pages will be prepared in manuscript.

Hour, Date, Place	Summary of Events and Information	Remarks and references to Appendices
24/4/15	[illegible]	
25/4/15	[illegible]	
26/4/15	[illegible] VLAMERTINGHE	[illegible]
27/4/15	[illegible]	[illegible]
28/4/15	[illegible]	[illegible]
29/4/15	[illegible]	[illegible]

WAR DIARY or INTELLIGENCE SUMMARY

Army Form C. 2118.

(1)

2nd Supply Train

Hour, Date, Place	Summary of Events and Information	Remarks and references to Appendices

30/4/15

Lieut Wells No 3 Coy was sent to North Sudan
Lieut Wallis found to be in hospital with wound in shoulder, this is now Confirmed by wire from the O i/c No 7 Stationary Hospital Boulogne.

General remarks:—

Since last diary was rendered the supply section of personnel Baggage has been concentrated, that is, it has been officered. The feeding of the R.F.A. among the recent operations around Ypres and have supported recently. This section has been under incessant shell fire for some considerable nights while delivering supplies between 10 pm and 15 am — The horses from April 23rd to 30th April being the worst.

The if. took wagons has again shown itself to be more than serviceable during this period of stress — on every night convoys the drivers displayed the greatest coolness although at times guides unable to manoeuvre all round some displayed, having to go forward sometimes distances before opportunity of a cross road, to turn at, was found — The carriage of spare wheels appears unlikely into. It they are has be strapped to the seat the stability of the seat is impaired, and become loose and springs and sockets give way.

The "Kay" wagon capacity is insufficient if they are fairly full generally in respects to be carried.

In addition to ordinary A.S.C. Transport + Supply duties the Divisional Train has been called upon during the last two weeks to Capital 6 jumpers in exceptional Services, such as R.E. Stores for trenches, bombs and shrapnel to + from has been supplies, fighting wounded, stretchers, and great pluck displayed by both Officers and men. TH

Signed [illegible] Col
28 April 1915
[illegible]

28th Division

28th Divisional Train

Vol V

WAR DIARY
or
INTELLIGENCE SUMMARY.
(Erase heading not required.)

Army Form C. 2118.

28 Divl Sigm

Hour, Date, Place	Summary of Events and Information	Remarks and references to Appendices
1/5/15	In camp Killino	7/258/ Dr O'Farrell M killed attached 82 Bath RFA
2/5/15	7/14/037/13 Dr Gray O.E. admitted to hospital wounded in foot. 2,3 yr employees move in new billets in Farm's Atred. 1 made West of Poperinghe. Ind AR Rawlins oysters from france & are prohibited	L/S dragon (S. service) attached at Jambetta. allright to receive field. 2,3 yr employees (Eyrels & Wilms) attach in new billet mentioned
3/5/15	No 1 company. Two coulericats drawn from Othele for 3 horses & 8 horses	1. HD horse $2 and no shot but 3/5/15
4/5/15		7/15R/3642 Dr Hack of interested R 5/5/15
5/5/15	36 ammunts received from OBHQ & issued to employees. 13 to HQ 3 8 to 2. 8 to 3 + 6 to 4r.	1. HD horse #20 could be shot bet 11/5/15
6/5/15	Nr fs dragon withdrawn from 12 London Regt & replaced by Wilms now supplies running to assist of workers - bar W.C M 1084 reported for duty on piece of bar very bay damaged. the following day show was one out of action through broken shell noses.	5 HD losses 3 any used to be shot bet 6/5/ c/MT 1282 Pte Johnson from 2 Camp #20 7.5.15. 7/14/045/7721 Pte Stewart M from D17 officers 5-5-15
7/5/15	SSM Ainstone reported for duty from Base Havre posted to 2 coy.	7/25R/0/713 Q/Sergt Logue 84
8/5/15	2 yr dragons and 156 gears to assist in the concentration of ammunition	7/14/037/31 Q/sergt Stoughtney 1st attd to Base "7/5/15
9/5/15	No 2 coy men reported for duty. Head Qrs company moved 6am - to new billet on Poperinghe - Ypres Rte. 1 mile S of Poperinghe. - two to new billet on Poperinghe - Vlamertinghe. handed over to 2 coy to complete	
10/5/15	15 waggons received from 12 London. handed over to 3 coy for like purpose. Have lost one dista to 3 coy for like purpose	

WAR DIARY
or
INTELLIGENCE SUMMARY.

(Erase heading not required.)

2/8 Bn London

Army Form C. 2118.

19

Hour, Date, Place	Summary of Events and Information	Remarks and references to Appendices
11/5/15	On arriving at Watou — Royal Scots introduced to French Mitrailleuse Coys. Company of 9 men drawn from here & posted to each company. No 1 to 4th Coy, No 2 to 2/24	7/2/2047 J. O. Fieldrich # Hahnutts'd P. 12/5/15
12/5/15		
13/5/15	One complete Lewis gun machine gun section received from 12 London Regt & handed over to 4th Coy as the M.G. section for the Battn. 7/Pvt. Pite M reports for duty. Lewis Machine Gun for Reserve Coys supplied by R.A.	
14/5/15	2 coy marches to new billets at MINNEZEELE & No coy to MOUTKERQUE	
15/5/15	Draft of 14 men arrive from base & posted to No 1 coy & Nos 2 Coy 2 line —	7/14/1037766 — 651 Murkay moved to regl at the coy request. 15/5/15 — 73/n#26 J. Lewis transfd unfit to Base army corps 14/5/15 7/14/37637 J cook J transfd to Base Army Supply Column 22/5/15 - 7/2 S.R. 6763 J Jackson G J gun apprenticed went back taken by L/Cpl A. 18/5/15
16/5/15	Orders received at Regthead for 4/5 Capt Mo. Hoyle, Jackson Wilberforce & Skelley proceed to England on Army Dispatch Service — DRAT Army — each two # Battalion of 3 coys. The Lancer from our Base stays draft C.O. & Bouthorn — C.U.C. proceed to England on Four days leave.	
17/5/15	3 drivers with 3 complete members horses were returned from 2/7 and from — sent to 2.b.S./Signal Rg RE	
18/5/15	Court martial on 2/Joulaine — 1 day Stopes exchanged for J.S. pattern	
19/5/15	Battn marches to Herzeele — Lettab stove — 12 Lewis rif Leave due complete with transport — No 11 coy armament 20 old billets at Peyperinghe	
20/5/15		
21/5/15	No 2 coy marches from Minneezeele to old billets near Peyperinghe — No 3 company advance to old billet near Peyperinghe from Herzeele	1 H.D. horse destroyed 7/2 J. 2/5/15

Army Form C. 2118.

WAR DIARY
or
INTELLIGENCE SUMMARY.
(Erase heading not required.)

28 Bay Squan

20

Instructions regarding War Diaries and Intelligence
Summaries are contained in F. S. Regs., Part II.
and the Staff Manual respectively. Title pages
will be prepared in manuscript.

Hour, Date, Place	Summary of Events and Information	Remarks and references to Appendices
22/5/15	In same billets. 2 HD remounts received & issued to Head Quarters sqn + 2 HD samples with u sqn transferred to Head Quarters sqn to replace casualties. Capt Griffin OC z sqn admitted to hospital suffering from influenza	1 HD horse destroyed #2 897 colic 2 hy 2 HD horses sent to rest camp 27/5/15 1 H.D. 1 HD horse destroyed
23/5/15		7/1/SR/577 D. Lucker Hospitalled HP 23/5/15 – 7/4/937 Sy D. Myre admitted HP 28/5/15 – 7/4/937 [21]
24/5/15		Sy Pelley + M Oy transferred to Base at Cyprus under age 27/5/15
25/5/15		
26/5/15	Lieut S. Rowlands RE Vet (IE) reported for duty + posted to E 2 sqn	7/801 St Bartlett Sy admitted HP 28/5/15 signed 1/5/15
27/5/15	Lieut T.W. Morrison- Harvard att. for duty at Hove. – 7/1441 2.S.M. Lyatt reported for duty + posted to HDt sqn – 2.S.M. Saxton transferred from Hdt 2s sqn to u sqn + 2.Lt J. Culford Ayres transferred from u sqn to HDt company. Lieut J.R. Sagarell + Lieut R.L. Turner reported for duty + posted to u + 2 company respectively	7/3761 St Hills J + 7/4/ St Langridge admitted HP 3-6 + 26-5/15 – 7/4/937 St.S.M. S. Brown RT admitted HP admitted in leave in England 15/5/15 Sentence
28/5/15	As 3 company move to Keupeule + 8 u Hole go into rest there – on 7/1/SR/11968 St Graham a. suspended –	
29/5/15	9.S. Hole came out of the trenches + billeted in square G4	1 R sent to Rest H Lee 2 bry 31/5/15 26/1/15
30/5/15	7/21/626 St Patrick FC having lost his mul so attacked to Head Zs bry + the matter reported to O/c ASC and on do Base	1 HD
31/5/15	1st Nev. Champion (Gill) bay Rd deft the division with its transport for 5C sqn. also 3s Nasty RHa with his transport for the 6th Curran. HDs company moves from site killet near Papermyles to billets 2 miles west of WATOO	

(73) W4141-463. 400,000. 9/14. H.&J. Ltd. Forms/C. 2118/10.

28th Division

25th Div: Train

Vol XI 2 — 30.6.15.

Army Form C. 2118.

WAR DIARY
or
INTELLIGENCE SUMMARY.
(Erase heading not required.)

28 Div train

21

Hour, Date, Place	Summary of Events and Information	Remarks and references to Appendices
2/6/15	4th horse killed	2 L.D horses received from RARE & carried to sick bay 1/6/15
3/6/15	65th Batty RHA 8th How Bde. Leave this morning & their transport on handed over to "B" echel train. New orders received from no Div. Handed over 84th Bde.	1 L.D horse used to tend sick on company 3/6/15
4/6/15	No 2 company with 83rd Bde marches from the old billet near POPERINGHE to WINNEZEELE & billets there	7/4/37780 Sr Rotholo) did PP 9/6/15 7/4/37532 Sr Jones) of dowsy 7/303544 Sr dowsy 7/4/3/899 Sr Smith W + 7/26071 S.Huff posted as qualified driving smiths 7/6/15
	No w company (Headquarters of company plus Blankets & baggage wagons) marches from the old billet near Poperinghe to HOUTKERQUE & billets there. The supply section under Lieut Austin accompanies the 85th Bde to LA CLYTE & remains there.	
5/6/15	Capt J.R Foster reports for duty & is posted to no 4 coy in relief of Capt Hawtrey	
6/6/15	Lieut Meiggrett & Pickweed reported for duty & posted to 2 company	
7/6/15	85th Bde Withdraws back from trenches to HOUTKERQUE Supply section rejoins company. Strong wind on Sr Leavitt, Harton, Huff & Kett	
8/6/15		
9/6/15		
10/6/15	Capt Hawtrey leaves for duty under D.A.D. Brekers & had stayed for duty in England. ll AD evacuates drivers from Lorry formery. for welch company	

WAR DIARY
or
INTELLIGENCE SUMMARY.
(Erase heading not required.)

Army Form C. 2118.

28 Divl Train

Hour, Date, Place	Summary of Events and Information	Remarks and references to Appendices
11/6/15	In some fields. Surplus transport from amalgamation of the Divisional Battalions transferred to Divl HT Depot under 2/Lieut Sargeaff. 2/Lieut Turner admitted to Hospital. Heavy fallen from his horse & badly sprained an ankle. 3 Company (64 sub) marched from HERZEELE to the front line S.W. of RENINGHELST — supply section fell. Come West.	1 HD A/57408 Pte to 1/4/FA to have removed. Rest surplus and MC Wd Sce. 14/037334 Dr Worley to No 2 HT Depot. 2 HD/9000 used to No 1 Section from Hop to 14/4/15. 1 Batr + 1 HD come to rest. See 1/6. LD ammunk supplies & rest. Rest from No 4 to 17/6/15. 14/037306 Dr Baggs Pte to No 2 HT Depot 17/6. See No 2 HT Depot. 14/037334 to Royal Horses transferred. Hop to dismtd 17 Depot 3/6/15. T4/37951 Pte H. Moorhead to 12/6/15. H/037740 to Depot. 13/6/15. T4/037743 to depot. Home Sup & Depot. 17/9/15. T4/037685 Pte Ricker sent to main unit. 7/3/1901 N Re. 14/037688 to Clearing H T/01 to depot.
12/6/15	Entered G. Harris B.S with a draft of 31st reinforcement from R.S.E & clearing command. Joined at Pont transferred from Hop to No 2 Co to requisitioning officer. Unknown transports no 1 Pats SD.	
13/6/15	One section engaged to WESTOUTRE. No 2 Co moved to M.H.C. (28) All above transferred to HT Pats as requisitioning officer.	19/6/15
14/6/15	Same H/w.	T4/037345 Dr Reggs discharged from HT 47 Migr west to Belgium 26.
15/6/15	Captain platoon from HQ on command to duplicate new Annex. H O.W. Sgeant transferred officer. Quel Lieut Base King reported from 4/Co to Amps to duty on duty.	Rest walks other than stated. 20/6/15.
16/6/15	Mad Ramdom to marched to WESTOUTRE supply section marked full with rank.	T/704 Dr Hutt & from 46 Div Train T/3240 Scorn H T/5343 Lillis R "Bentley" from front relief Reg P
17/6/15	In same billets	
19.6.15	No D Coy moved from billets MRJ 23 to WESTOUTRE M9C.15 Supply Section and not move with the unit. Major Lea P.G.R. Kept command of the Train.	
20.6.15	No III Coy moved from billet M6C.5 to M14 6.1.2. Supply section and not move with the unit. No IV Coy moved billet from WATOU to M.8.C.9.1. The Supply Section moved with the unit. No II Coy moved billet HQ Coy sec 3 G.S wagons, 6 HD Ambces these waves activity D.T. 4.9.12. HD Ansct new billets to replace HT Des T4/03957 Sowe W T4/037826 Rooney P to 1/6 Middlesex Reg T4/037648 Wenn A T/3052 Dodsley. We section for these three Coys moving to new billets tomorrow. Rest of the Divisional artillery had orders to replace HT Dec near to the artillery
	2 Coys nos I & III were too near to the artillery	

WAR DIARY
or
INTELLIGENCE SUMMARY

(Erase heading not required.)

Army Form C. 2118.

23

XXVII DIVISIONAL TRAIN – WESTOUTRE

Hour, Date, Place	Summary of Events and Information	Remarks and references to Appendices
21.6.15"	Five horses were cast by DADR, when visiting 28th Division for that purpose, four were H.D. horses & one was L.D. reason being that they were unmanageable. Six H.D. horses were obtained from 3rd Divisional Ammunition Column at GR.6.B.64 by order of DADR & were allotted to H.Q. & N°2, H.H.D & N°1 Coy. — Billets remain as same place.	Cast. 2 H.D. from No 2 Coy. 1 L.D.S. 1 H.D. from No 3 Coy 1 H.D. from H.Q Coy H.H.D. to H.Q. Coy 2 H.D. to No 2 Coy. Driver Groom to joint scheme 21/4/15
9.30 AM 22.6.15"	No II Coy moved billets at WESTOUTRE to M7.a.5.1, on BAILLEUL Road — Eight N.C.O.s when arrived from Base Horse Transport Depot Shorncliffe, & one of which were to replace clerks & Shetland writers were allotted as follows: — four men to No 1 Coy — One man to No 3 Coy — Three men to No 2 Coy	kent Schultz from hospital 29/6/15 arrivals 22/6/15 340. 720837 Seabert T jun D° 722267 Oxley T D° 781749 Niles E Base D° 724542 85 Davis H D° Bateswell Christiani } from H.Q. T Depot Shorncliffe
23.6.15	Three N.C.O.s & men left the Train for Base Horse Transport Depot. All billets remain in same places.	
24.6.10"	Billets same as previous day, one Officer Lieut Saybell admitted to hospital. Three men arrived from Base Inclamfort Depot for duty with the train & were posted one each to H.Q Coy No II Coy & No III Coy.	7/27892 D° Connelly P 2603 " Teagle D 7/24037 " Young C Departures 23/6/15 D° Kratos to hospital D° Donny } to remain Base D° Nowson } D° Pierce Wm (M. Lewis 24/4/15 Lieut H.Saybell adm. to H.P 24/6/15
25.6.15 Friday.	No changes.	
26.6.15 Saturday.	No Changes. 2 Surplus Cooks were transferred to Royal Flanders & 2nd East Surrey Regt	7/30034 "Dooley E

(9 29 6) W.14141—483. 100,000 9/14 H W V Forms/C. 2118/10

Army Form C. 2118.

WAR DIARY
or
INTELLIGENCE SUMMARY.
(Erase heading not required.)

of XXVIII DIVISIONAL TRAIN, WESTHOUTRE.

Hour, Date, Place	Summary of Events and Information	Remarks and references to Appendices
SUNDAY 27.6.15.	Everything quiet – Billets in same place – Belgium interpreter of No IV Coy admitted to hospital at BAILLEUL. CO visited 8th Division re reference 16 Hay wagons of 8th Brigade.	
MONDAY 28.6.15.	Billets in same place. One Limbered G.S. Wagon to 5th Division & one water cart to 3rd Brigade ammunition Column 5th Division. Both were in possession of No IV Coy. Three surplus from 8th Middlesex Regt. Three hay wagons on loan to 8th Brigade returned to HQ of Coy.	
TUESDAY 29.6.15	Twenty four G.S. wagons required daily – until further orders – by Royal Engineers for road repairs – authority 2nd Corps/G.C. 779. It has been decided to collect ten wagons from HQ of Coy, six from No IV & four from No III Coys & part them at Headquarters Coy under Capt Reynolds who will detail them daily & report on damage done on this daily. One reading lense from HQ Coy to 85th Brigade for issue to 2nd K.O.R.L. Regt. Three G.S. wagons (baggage wagons) received from 366, 45 & 62 Batteries R.F.A. The Commanding Officer Major Lea & Suspected No II & No III Coys – Vincent. Marching Order dismounted. All available men were inspected. Two field kitchens returned from 1st Welsh Regt & 2nd Northumberland Fusiliers.	
WEDNESDAY 30.6.15.		

[signature] Major
1.7.15

28th Division

61/6292

28th Divisional Train

Vol VII

July 15

One

Army Form C. 2118.

WAR DIARY
OR
INTELLIGENCE SUMMARY.
(Erase heading not required.)

of XXVIII DIVISIONAL TRAIN WESTOUTRE

Instructions regarding War Diaries and Intelligence Summaries are contained in F.S. Regs., Part II. and the Staff Manual respectively. Title pages will be prepared in manuscript.

Hour, Date, Place	Summary of Events and Information	Remarks and references to Appendices
THURSDAY JULY 1ST 1915	The wagons G.S. which became surplus owing to the with drawal of the mot Beaver wagons were redistributed as follows. To 5" DIVISION 22 G.S. wagons, 21 heavy draught horses, 12 Drivers. To infantry Brigades 14 G.S. wagons, 28 heavy draught horses (these replaced 14 limbered G.S. cook carts). To 50" DIVISION one G.S. wagon, two heavy draught horses. Two drivers. To 28" Field Coy R.E. one G.S. wagon (to make up deficiency). To 50" DIVISIONAL TRAIN two limbered G.S. wagons & to the R.F.A. twelve limbered G.S. wagons These were the surplus with drawn from 83rd, 85rd & 84 Brigades.	
FRIDAY 2.7.15.	Four field kitchens received from 5" DIVISIONAL TRAIN. Two L.D horses returned from 5" DIVISIONAL TRAIN as unserviceable & will be sent to the Mobile vet Section.	
SATURDAY 3.7.15.	Four field kitchens dispatched to 2" EAST YORKS, 1st YORKS & LANCS 3 Royal DUBLIERS & 3" MIDDLESEX as complete divisionals with the exception of horses. One full kitchen complete returned to no1 Company from 2" East Yorks. The front portion Horse & harness of a field kitchen returned from Fort rouges R.g.F. One G.S. wagon returned from 31st Brigade R.F.A. One field kitchen returned to host Coy from 3" MIDDLESEX	
SUNDAY 4.7.15.	Lieut Sargent J.R. retained from hospital. S4/090714 Pt Bryant A.G. arrived from Base & posted to no 3 Coy. One of the men attached to no1 Coy from 3" MIDDLESEX Ran amot. S4/43753 Sgt Adam M.C. Lut. no3 Coy for A.G's office Base.	
MONDAY 5.7.15.	Two limbered G.S. wagons received from 49" Div Train.	

Army Form C. 2118.

WAR DIARY
INTELLIGENCE SUMMARY.
(Erase heading not required.)

of XXVIII DIVISIONAL TRAIN WESTOUTRE

Hour, Date, Place	Summary of Events and Information	Remarks and references to Appendices
TUESDAY 6.7.15.	One travelling kitchen received from 3rd MIDDLESEX REGT & passed on to 3rd ROYAL FUSILIERS. Dr GOLDSMITH of H.Q. Coy admitted to hospital.	
WEDNESDAY 7.7.15.	One limbered G.S. wagon to 3rd Royal FUSILIERS & one to BUFFS both from no III Coy. Sgt WILLMOTT's riders found on field next to 3rd Brigade of Gunners.	
THURSDAY 8.7.15.	Twenty one surplus drivers sent to BASE HORSETRANSPORT DEPÔT ¼ of Capt GUTHRIE via BAILLEUL.	
FRIDAY 9.7.15.	Three G.S. wagons, One Cooker, One limbered G.S. & 5 drivers - all surplus - sent to BASE HORSETRANSPORT DEPÔT by road under LIEUT. LEVEY. Two L.D. horses & one rider to mobile vet'sect. Two drivers sent from hospital. The twenty five wagons on R.E. work are also required every night to take Belgian workmen, who are employed in digging trenches from WESTOUTRE to DICKEBUSH. The C.R.A. is to find the horses whenever wagons parade at 4 p.m. & return at 3.30 a.m. 10/7/15. The officer in charge journal by 28th Divn Train.	
SATURDAY 10.7.15.	One ridden & one L.D. horse to mobile vet'sect - two miles from 2nd K.O.R. Lancs. Instructions received that The train is to move back to near BERTHEN as it is concluded that there is too much transport & scarcity of water near the front line.	
SUNDAY 11.7.15.	All pollen transport is being moved back to WESTOUTRE area. CO visits BERTHEN & selects three billets as suitable for no II, III r IV Coys - SSO's Can methoris an accident CO visits no II r IV Coys 1/19 & Van Dreven Bentley T.S. Burnavick 14 days F.P. no I. Church parade held at no billet for all Coys. The Gunners provided an officer to take service to DICKEBUSH with Belgian workers	

Army Form C. 2118.

WAR DIARY
or
INTELLIGENCE SUMMARY.
(Erase heading not required.)

XXVII DIVISIONAL TRAIN WESTOUTRE

27

Instructions regarding War Diaries and Intelligence Summaries are contained in F.S. Regs., Part II. and the Staff Manual respectively. Title pages will be prepared in manuscript.

Hour, Date, Place	Summary of Events and Information	Remarks and references to Appendices
MONDAY. 12.7.15	No 3 Coy ordered to move to new billets at BERTHEN – Supply Section moves with Coy. O.C. looked out for billets for Headquarters & Train. Lieut Levy Rec. returned from T. HERONVAL having handed over surplus transport total. Orders issued to No II & IV Coys to move to new billets. One mule sent to 2nd K.O.R. Lancs.	MAP BELGIUM 27. 1:40000 R.2.2.C.2.E.
TUESDAY. 13.7.15	Lieut Austin granted 5 days leave. No 2 Coy moved to new billets R15.E.D. No 4 Coy moved to new billets R15.D.1.4. The Supply Section moved with Companies. L/Cpl Gethin returned from leave.	BELGIUM. 27/1:40000 R23G.5.B.
WEDNESDAY. 14.7.15	Headquarters Coy moved to new billets. Orders issued to return 84 & 85 Brigade baggage waggons which are on R.E. work.	
THURSDAY. 15.7.15	One saddle horse transferred to 84th Field Ambulance, one M.D. horse to 38 Field Coy R.E., one M.D. horse to Surrey Yeomanry, 5 mules to 3rd Brigade RFA, 2 mules to 146th Brigade RFA, 12 mules 31st Brigade RFA, 3 mules to 8 Brigade RFA, One rider to 85 Brigade, one LD 67th Leeds Regt T One pack pony to 2nd Buffs. The waggons which carry the Belgium workers to DICKEBUSH will discontinue doing so until further orders.	
FRIDAY. 16.7.15	No Changes –	
SATURDAY. 17.7.15	Headquarters of the Divisional Train moved from WESTOUTRE Village to R16 D.7.6.	REF BELGIUM 27. 1:40000
SUNDAY. 18.7.15	No Changes. 1/c Royal Irish Regt joined 80 Div Train baggage waggons handed over to No 3 Coy	

Army Form C. 2118.

WAR DIARY
or
INTELLIGENCE SUMMARY.
(Erase heading not required.)

XXVIII DIVISIONAL TRAIN

Hour, Date, Place	Summary of Events and Information	Remarks and references to Appendices
MONDAY 19.7.15	The following changes have taken place:— Capt Yoska to command No 4 Coy, Lt Williams from No 4 Coy to H.Q Coy. Lt Levy from H.Q Coy to ~~supernumerary officer No 4 Coy~~ ~~Lt Robins from supernumerary officer to~~ ~~Williams~~ No 4 Coy to Transport Officer ~~No 4 Coy~~ Lt Saywell from transport officer No 4 Coy to Coy Lt Schultz from requisitioning officer No 4 Coy to Supply Officer No 4 Coy. Arms inspection for Headquarters & Train	
TUESDAY 20.7.15	One L.D. & three H.D horses from artillery. One L.D. & 3 pack firers from Yeomanry, all baggage wagons to R.E. work again with Head Quarters Co. 1 L.D from 3.6 to Cheshire Regt. 12 H.D from H.Q Co to No 4 Coy. Aeroplane flashlight 41 H.D from H.Q Co to 2nd Ind Amm Column	
WEDNESDAY 21.7.15	Surplus hay wagon from H.Q.Co handed to 3.6 for delivery to 4th Welch Regt. An exchange for a cooker, which was sent to Railhead. One horse seriously injured for R.E. work. D Crosts awarded in day No 1.	
THURSDAY 22.7.15		
FRIDAY 23.7.15	OC ~~55~~ with Capt Park inspected 1st line transport of 84th Brigade	
SATURDAY 24.7.15	2nd in command. Regt. left the 28th Division	
SUNDAY 25.7.15	Lt King & CSM Bycott returned off leave 3.30 am	
MONDAY 26.7.15	One horse of H.Q Coy shot on account of injuries received. One acct of Lt Saywell & three men left on leave for England	
TUESDAY 27.7.15	Orderly room to 30 cases of ammunition for Wednesday	
WEDNESDAY 28.7.15	All surplus horses to be at Headquarti Coy by 10.30 am for Veterinary inspection reclassification. Distribution as follows:— 1 pack wry H.D to H.Q Coy, 2 L.D. + mule to No 2 Coy. 3 H.D. to No 3 Coy	

Forms/C. 2118/10

Army Form C. 2118.

29

WAR DIARY
or
INTELLIGENCE SUMMARY.
(Erase heading not required.)

XXVII DIVISIONAL TRAIN

Instructions regarding War Diaries and Intelligence Summaries are contained in F.S. Regs., Part II. and the Staff Manual respectively. Title pages will be prepared in manuscript.

Hour, Date, Place	Summary of Events and Information	Remarks and references to Appendices
WEDNESDAY 28.7.15	4 Pack ponies to Horse Coy. - One horse ordered to be shot by 6 Secn. to Mobile Vet Sect.	
THURSDAY 29.7.15	17 tents for new billets dumps in case of move.	
FRIDAY 30.7.15	Capt Williams RAVC returned to duty. One G.S.wagon to Horse Coy from East Surreys	
SATURDAY 31.7.15	OC looks for new billets. Driver Nagle reported from Base for duty reported to No 4.O Coy	

121/6857

28th Division

28th Divl: Train
Vol VIII
August 15.

WAR DIARY
of
INTELLIGENCE SUMMARY.

(Erase heading not required.)

Army Form C. 2118.

XXVIII DIVISIONAL TRAIN

AUGUST 1915

Hour, Date, Place	Summary of Events and Information	Remarks and references to Appendices
SUNDAY AUGUST 1st 1915	Lt Sagwell & 3 N.C.O.'men returned from leave. One limbered G.S. wagon received from Monmouth Regt.	
MONDAY " 2 "	Two H.D. horses received from 3rd Brigade R.F.A. One L.D. horse to 8th Brigade. Capt Foster & 3 N.C.O.'men left on leave – C.O. a.d.c. & O.C. H.Q.	
TUESDAY " 3 "	Visited new billets proposed to be occupied by Host Company. No I, III & IV Coys visited & instructed to make certain that Motor transport was correct & return required by Friday.	
WEDNESDAY " 4 "	Wet. A.D.M.S. inspected all the supplies stores in the train at H.Q. Company. Two riding & one L.D. & one Packhorse were sent to Mobile Veterinary Section. One L.D. sent to 1st Welsh Regt. One L.D. to 638th Div Signals. One H.D. to 86 Field Ambulance. Three L.D. to H.Q. Coy for re distribution. Two L.D. to III Company. One L.D. to IV Coy. Two Clergymen from 28th Div Headquarters received by H.Q. Coy.	
THURSDAY " 5 "	O.C. visited railhead. 8 G.S. wagons to POPPERINGHE on coal fatigue for Sanitary Section. Seven Packhorses inspected by D.D.R. in field South of WESTOUTRE & were ordered to be sent to Field Remount Section at CAESTRE. Inspection of new billet for train Headquarters by O.C.	

WAR DIARY
or
INTELLIGENCE SUMMARY.
(Erase heading not required.)

Army Form C. 2118.

XXVIII DIVISIONAL TRAIN

AUGUST 1915

Hour, Date, Place	Summary of Events and Information	Remarks and references to Appendices
FRIDAY. AUGUST 6 1915.	ADJ'T & OC inspected all 1st line transport & field ambulances reclassified the horses. W.O. Weston returned to H Company for duty. W.O. Houghton A/ detached for R.E. Road repair sent.	
SATURDAY. 7 "	Two heavy draught horses from King's Own Royal Lancs. One rider from Yorks Lancers. Two riders to Surrey Yeomanry.	
SUNDAY. 8 "	One horse Company G 34th Div. Train attached whilst 110 Brigade are with The 28th Division. The Adjutant proceeded out their Billet & refilling point. O.C. also visited the Company. Capt. Jostes & two men returned off leave.	
MONDAY. 9th "	Lt Denny & two men left on leave. OC inspects all refilling points & visited G.HQ. on duty. Assistant to BAILLEUL to meet Capt Hannay who is posted to Train for instruction.	
TUESDAY. 10th "	Three days for instruction. No Changes.	
WEDNESDAY. 11th "	Ration question raised by OC Headquarters Company owing to shortage of rations for the horses. Capt Hannay leaves the Train for England.	
THURSDAY. 12.	No Changes.	
FRIDAY 13	OC instructed wheeler proposed Headquarters of Train at WESTOUTRE. OC visits the Companies & arrange with DA.C. to exchange	

WAR DIARY
or INTELLIGENCE SUMMARY. XXVII DIVISIONAL TRAIN.

(Erase heading not required.)

Army Form C. 2118.

Instructions regarding War Diaries and Intelligence Summaries are contained in F.S. Regs., Part II. and the Staff Manual respectively. Title pages will be prepared in manuscript.

Hour, Date, Place	Summary of Events and Information	Remarks and references to Appendices
FRIDAY AUGUST 13th 1915.	Westoutre HQ closed with Train.	
SATURDAY 14th 1915.	Train Headquarters moves to WESTOUTRE. Billeting certificate given to Maire of BOSCHEPE for billets evacuated. 1st Line transport visited by O.C. & Adjutant	
SUNDAY 15th 1915.	Lt DENNY. 2nd Divn Train returns off leave. Instruction to 2 Company that No Supply wagons of the civils in 84th Brigade would not be required as the Supply Column would dump at 1st Line Transport. 84th Brigade Refilling from 1st Line. 19 HD horses are being exchanged at D.A.C. as follows: 10 HD from 1 Company 3 from 3 Company 3 from 6th Welsh 2 from Northumberland Fusiliers from Royal Fusiliers. O.C. (Major Lea) & Capt Reynolds & one man depart on leave. One Orderlies from base posted to 2 Company. 6 Drivers from base for Monmouth transport posted to	
MONDAY. 16th 1915.	No 2 Coy & 1 Coy. Adjutant left by car Western for VlenTHEROUANNE. Lt Dixon & Adjutant left by car Western for 28th Division - arrived THEROUANNE. 6 late open 1st Line transport for 85th Division. Adjutant left 5.30am 2.20 pm Transport had not arrived. Adjutant left 5.30am with Car for Train Headquarters.	
TUESDAY 17		

Army Form C. 2118.

WAR DIARY
or
INTELLIGENCE SUMMARY.   28th DIVISIONAL TRAIN   WESTOUTRE
(Erase heading not required.)

Instructions regarding War Diaries and Intelligence Summaries are contained in F.S. Regs., Part II and the Staff Manual respectively. Title pages will be prepared in manuscript.

Hour, Date, Place	Summary of Events and Information	Remarks and references to Appendices
WEDNESDAY AUG 18th 1915	15 Drivers left by motor lorry for Rest Camp THEROUANNE to bring up 28th Divn transport as the conveying drivers were not allowed to proceed further that rest camp.	
THURSDAY 19th 1915	Lt Gatti, seven NCO's & one wagon left 8 am for THEROUANNE to bring up transport for the 3rd MONMOUTH Regt. Eight wagons detailed for Coal fatigue. Coal required by Cavalry Sections at WESTOUTRE, LOCRE & DRANOUTRE for latter. 13 HD horses drawn from RHC for replacing casualties in 1st Line transport. Lt Drew returned from THEROUANNE with 4 GS wagons, 13 Coys Carts, 1 Maltese Cart & 3 Travelling Kitchens to bring to GHQ relieving 5pm.	
FRIDAY 20th 1915	+Transport from THEROUANNE handed over to 6 1st Line.	
SATURDAY 21st 1915	NO REPORT. All surplus transport being handed into the Train.	
SUNDAY 22nd 1915	Spare limbered wagons of the Artillery returned to Train. Lt Gatti returned from THEROUANNE with 1st Line transport for 3/Monmouth Regt. Four mules drawn from Remount Depot CHESTRE by 4 Coy RFC.	
MONDAY 23rd 1915	Major Lea returned off leave One NCO, 3/Monmouth took over 4 limbered G.S. wagons 1 Mess Cart, 1 GS wagon, 15 LD horses 2 HD horses.	Lt Peters & two others left on leave
TUESDAY 24th 1915	Capt Reynolds returned off leave. 10 limbered G.S. wagons 96 LD horses 4 mules handed over to 50th Divisional Train at Map 36 B 22. a. 4.6. Convoy left 8.30 am i/c of a NCO from 3 Coy returned with receipt. C.O. Capt Reynolds visited Selit proposed	
WEDNESDAY 25 1915	Train H.Q. Company. One wagon GS left to OC. ag:ng party to move kits stores to DRANOUTRE for H.Q. Company. H.Q. Company moves from present billet to M 32. B. 57k.	

WAR DIARY or INTELLIGENCE SUMMARY. XXVIII DIVISIONAL TRAIN

(Erase heading not required.)

Army Form C. 2118.

WESTOUTRE

Hour, Date, Place	Summary of Events and Information	Remarks and references to Appendices
AUGUST.		
WEDNESDAY 25. 1915	Owing to shortage of water & new Supply arrangements & dumping at £ line Supply section did not move out. Main Company but also part of Divisional Transport Supply dumps or refilling point moved to M.33.a.7.7.	
THURSDAY. 26. 1915	Inspection of HQ Company Nos 2.3 & 4 by G.O.C. 28th Division & others. Ordered with the exception of one pair sent to be used for baggage wagon No. 3. That the Train was to draw felt tails from ordnance. 2.30 pm Adjutant with 1NCO & two drivers left by car for THEROUANNE to collect 3 water carts complete – two for HQ Company & one for Y/Monmouth Regt now for 49th Heavy Howitzer Brigade. All surplus horses sent to HQ Company – inspected by ADVS – rechecked.	
FRIDAY 27. 1915	Two RD vans riders sent to 2nd K.O.Y.L.I. Eight RD. Three pack & one mule sent to Y/Monmouth regiment. BC held orderly room at HQ Company. Nos 2 & 3 Company. Driver Martin attached to HQ Train sent to Hospital. 19 HD horses drawn from DAC. Two water carts collected by Y/Monmouth Regt.	
SATURDAY 28. 1915		
SUNDAY. 29. 1915	Twenty one ED dragoons to L'ABEELE for coal. T.4-037661 Segt Newens. T.4-037766 Sergt Newbury. 037644 Cpl Stissett 037539 Cpl Mahon. 037539 Cpl Thomas. 037680 Pt Worrall leave for England to take up duties with new Army as Asst & Adjutant next to lens. H.Y.st & 3rd Monmouth Regiment.	
MONDAY 30. 1915		
TUESDAY 31. 1915	O.C. & A/ visits all Companies & also 1st 2nd & 3rd Monmouth Regiments. No changes	

121/7/00

28th Division

28th Divl: Train
Vol IX
Sept. 15

WAR DIARY or INTELLIGENCE SUMMARY. XXVIII DIVISIONAL TRAIN

WESTOUTRE

Army Form C. 2118.

Hour, Date, Place	Summary of Events and Information	Remarks and references to Appendices
SEPTEMBER WEDNESDAY 1ST 1915	Eight wagons on Coal fatigue for Sanitary Sections at WESTOUTRE, LOCRE & DRANOUTRE. Cond. ABYSS from HQ Company to Train HQ. 2nd Lt Duff returned to duty. O.C. v/Lt Denny to YPERQUINNE to see 2nd Cav Corps re claims. No changes.	
THURSDAY 2ND 1915	O.C. v/Call to No 2 Company attending Orderly room. No changes	
FRIDAY 3RD 1915	Twenty one G.S. wagons to POPPERINGHE on Coal fatigue - to be allowed at No 3 Company refilling point. C.O. Ambrose in charge	
SATURDAY 4TH "	Same fatigue on same number of wagons in site. Lt Coleman + two drivers returned off leave. Two RD horses handed over to 6th Welsh Regt from 3 Company. One HD horse to 9th Bat King's Own	
SUNDAY 5TH "	One Rifles transferred from 3 Coy to HQ. Coy.	
MONDAY 6TH "	X-keys red with ten GS wagons for coal to Batter. W/O Ambrose with seven wagons to Brush Coal fatigue - Capt Boole + two other ranks depart on leave. O.C. v/Day visits 6th WELSH Regts 1st Line transport also to BAILLEUL to see cahebels at billet of Sanitary Sect.	
TUESDAY 7TH "	Twenty one wagons G.S. on Coal fatigue to POPPERINGHE - Lt Coleman i/c O.C. v/All looking for new billets- All round 6th WELSH Regt.	
WEDNESDAY 8TH "	No changes.	
THURSDAY 9 "	BOSCHEPPE ROAD - C.O. inspected New Company marching order - Seven wagons from No 2 Company under W/O Ambrose to POPPERINGHE for Coal	Train Headquarters moved from WESTOUTRE to new billet on WESTOUTRE Rd. MAP 27. R.16.d.55.

Army Form C. 2118.

WAR DIARY
or
INTELLIGENCE SUMMARY.
(Erase heading not required.)

XXVIII DIVISIONAL TRAIN

Instructions regarding War Diaries and Intelligence Summaries are contained in F.S. Regs., Part II. and the Staff Manual respectively. Title pages will be prepared in manuscript.

Hour, Date, Place	Summary of Events and Information	Remarks and references to Appendices
SEPTEMBER		
FRIDAY 10" 1916	O.C. AA+QMG. ADVS inspected 1st Line transport of 85th Brigade.	
SATURDAY 11" 1915	To Austin with twenty one wagons to POPPERINGHE on Coal fatigue.	
SUNDAY 12" 1915	To Coleman with twenty one wagons to POPPERINGHE on Coal fatigue.	
	To Roy with fifteen wagons to POPPERINGHE on Coal fatigue. O. visits all Companies	Departures
	O.C. visits room at H Company. Four other ranks to B.H.T. Depot to join Handcthan.	7/25R/019441 P/Sgt Morgan A
	Seven other ranks join them from base.	T/4/037530 P/Cpl Hodges 037660 P/Cpl Taylor 4 T/3/1673 P/Cpl Yuntin R.
MONDAY 13"	Eight wagons on Coal fatigue for battn at WESTOUTRE - LOCRE - DRANOUTRE.	Arrivals.
	Seven wagons Carting bricks for 83rd Brigade from PONT-DE-NIEPPE to LOCRE.	
TUESDAY 14"	D.A.M.R. in charge of Convoy.	
	Lt Leony whe Newport Carting bricks from PONT-DE-NIEPPE for H.Q. Company.	
	At Doulieu with Convoy of 15wagons to POPPERINGHE on Coal fatigue.	
WEDNESDAY 15"	O.C. G.S.R. Brigade to arrange for fatigue parties to tint wagons on brick work	
	One wagon + eleven centers from 4 Company - 3 wagons - 6 centers from 2 Company	
	6 wagons + 3 centers from 3 Company ; 6 wagons + 3 centers from 2 Company	
	All on Carting bricks for 84 Brigade + Train - 1st Convoy leaves D.H.Q. 7am.	
	2d ST BERTHEN. 8am. fatigue part supplied by D1 Brigade. Out wind inspects	
	Convoys before leaving. C.O. visits billets at PONT-DE-NIEPPE.	
THURSDAY 16"	2 wagons + 4 leaders from HQ Coy. - 2 wagons + 4 leaders from II Coy. - 3 wagons 3 leaders	
	from III Coy - 3 wagons 3 leaders + 4 officers from IV Company Carting bricks from	
	PONT-DE-NIEPPE to HQ Company + on base for E&S SURREY YEO.	
	C.O. DA+QMG inspects 1st Line transport of 85 Brigade. Holds orderly room.	
FRIDAY 17"	at HQ Company 2.30 pm.	
	Lt Coleman with Convoy of Y Company + wagon + 10 DAC to PONT-DE-NIEPPE brick frales	
	for bricks for 85 Brigade. fatigue party provided by 85th Brigade - all return	
	in the train Cancelled. O.C. visits all Companies.	

WAR DIARY or INTELLIGENCE SUMMARY.

Army Form C. 2118.

XXVIII Divisional Train.

(Erase heading not required.)

Hour, Date, Place	Summary of Events and Information	Remarks and references to Appendices
SEPTEMBER		
SATURDAY. 18th 1915.	CO. & DAQMG. inspected 1st line transport of 83 Brigade. All Companies in Train on route march. Adjutant visits 1st line transport about 1st line transport.	
SUNDAY 19th 1915.	No Changes – 33 Bell tents handed over to the Manlui Brigades.	
MONDAY 20th "	OC in Company with SSO visits new area. Company Commanders parade at Train Headquarters 3pm – Subject marching out of present area around WESTOUTRE 6	
TUESDAY 21st "	new area at MERRIS. No 2 Company move ? to new area – BORRE – Gain, angers & Supply (empty) moved supply sections of Train at 8 am; baggage section at 1 pm after mules had rested	Company id reft in their new area on arrival
WEDNESDAY 22nd "	No 4 Company moved at 8 am to new area STRAZEELE. Wain, angers & Supply Sect (empty) – baggage section moved at 1 pm after 83rd Brigade. Lt. E.H. Browne joined the Train from Nr Depot. Have posted to his Company Certificate of billets. Train HQ is given as Mme. Botcliffe.	#Company STRAZEELE BORE
THURSDAY 23rd "	No 2 Company moved to new area OUTERSTIENE – Company & Supply angers (empty) from billets at 8 am – baggage section at 1 pm with 82nd Brigade. Train Headquarters move from billets at 9.45 am to St JEAN CAPPELE Head Qrs & Company move at 8.30 am to St JEAN CAPPELE Train Headquarters & HQ Company move from St JEAN CAPPELE	2 " OUTERSTIENE HQ Coy MERRIS THURSDAY 23rd SEPT. 1915. Lieut BROWNE transferred from No II Company to No III Company.
FRIDAY. 24th "	When all MERRIS – arrive at 12.30 noon – OC. visits all companies. The Train replies at 9 am & also at 4.30 pm in future with remain in possession of rations for the following day.	
SATURDAY. 25	CO. DAQMG. & ADVS. inspect armaments for 28th Division. Orders received that the Division would move to MERVILLE. Order of march. No 2 Company – HQ Train & HQ Company – No 3 Company – hort Company. Baggage wagons to march with while supply wagons with Companies.	

Army Form C. 2118.

WAR DIARY
or
INTELLIGENCE SUMMARY.
(Erase heading not required.)

XXVIII DIVISION AL TRAIN

Instructions regarding War Diaries and Intelligence Summaries are contained in F. S. Regs., Part II. and the Staff Manual respectively. Title pages will be prepared in manuscript.

Hour, Date, Place	Summary of Events and Information	Remarks and references to Appendices
SUNDAY SEPT 26th 1915	28th DIVISION moves to BETHUNE to following in order of march. 1. HDQ Company from OUTERSTEINE 9 am to ROBECQ 4.30 pm Baggage wagons with 83rd Brigade: Supply wagons with Company. 2. Train & DHSA from MERRIS 7.30 am to BETHUNE 7 pm Baggage wagons with Divisional troops: Supply wagons with Company 3. No 3 Company from BORRE 9 am to CORNE-MALO (at bottom of C in CORNE-MALO) on the MERVILLE-HIVGE road (met Headquarters 3rd) Baggage wagons with 84 Brigade - Supply wagons with Company 4. No 4 Company from STRAZEELE 9.40 am to Station in BETHUNE 8 pm Baggage wagons with 85 Brigade & Supply wagons with Company	put MAP 36B. E16A.
MONDAY SEPT 27th 1915.	All Train Companies moved as follows Headquarters Company from BETHUNE to farm on BETHUNE-BRUAY No 2 Company from ROBECQ to Same No 3 Company from BORRE to Same No 4 Company from BETHUNE to Same All Baggage & Supply wagons returned to their Companies Refilling points immediately south of railway crossing on the BETHUNE-BRUAY road. HQ Company refilling RB troops Headquarters of Train moved from 15 Rue de GAMBETTA to Rue de ESPLANADE located by DIVISIONAL HQRS.	
TUESDAY SEPT 28th 1915.		
WEDNESDAY SEPT 29th 1915.	Companies & refilling points located. First reinforcement despatched to their units. Orders for Train Companies to move from their present billets received 2.30 pm. follows :- new billets found Companies move at	

Army Form C. 2118.

WAR DIARY
or
INTELLIGENCE SUMMARY.
(Erase heading not required.)

XXVIII DIVISIONAL TRAIN

Hour, Date, Place	Summary of Events and Information	Remarks and references to Appendices
WEDNESDAY SEPT. 29th 1915	Headquarter Company from E16A to E3D4Y. No 2 Company from do to E4Y5. No 3 Company from do to E4A59. No 4 Company from do to E4A05. Move completed 9.30pm 29.9.15. Refilling points on road E4A&5	Ref MAP 36.10.
THURSDAY SEPT 30th 1915	E3D3Y. OC. used refilling points with Train Companies. Thirty two machine Guns - 18 Limbers G.S. wagons 36 L.D. horses & 18 drivers taken over from 9th Division & posted with H.Q. Company	[signature] FM for ytea army 28th Dn Tren. 1/10/15.
FRIDAY OCT 1st 1915		

12/7519

28th Division

28th Div Train

Oct 1915

Vol X

Army Form C. 2118.

WAR DIARY
or
INTELLIGENCE SUMMARY.
(Erase heading not required.)

XXVIII DIVISIONAL TRAIN   39.

Hour, Date, Place	Summary of Events and Information	Remarks and references to Appendices
OCTOBER FRIDAY 1st 1915.	32 Machine Guns – 18 Limbered G.S. wagons 361 D Horses – 18 Officers of 9th Division handed over to Headquarters 28th Division by the train. One G.S. wagon two HD horses taken over from 9th Division it being the Supply wagon of the 3rd Brigading Train	
SATURDAY 2nd	One limber complete with two L Horses received from 9th Div Train. The following reinforcements sent to join their units. 2 Officers. 376 O.Ranks. Baggage wagons sent up to first line transport. Refilling of supply wagons to take place in the afternoon.	
SUNDAY 3rd	No supply replacements to join their regiments this Officers their standards. Train headquarters move from One d'esplanade to another part of BETHUNE. Stopping to call place in the evening. Supply wagons will leave for 1st line transport train. Summary of evidence taken in case of Corporal Robertson 3 Coy Reinforcements sent up to 1st line as follows. Officers 8 Other Ranks 24	
MONDAY 4th	Summary of evidence taken in case of Ds keage – using threatening language to a Superior Officer. All train Officers to Headquarters of Train orders received that Division will move on 6th inst	
TUESDAY 5th		
WEDNESDAY 6th	Reinforcements to 1st line Officers 6 O.Ranks 107. HQ Company does not move. HQ.1,3.Train moves from BETHUNE to BUSNES dep 7.30 am arr 1.30 pm. No.II Company moves from BETHUNE to	Ref MAP 36A. P 20-26-31-32. " 12.30 noon arr.

Army Form C. 2118.

40

WAR DIARY
or
INTELLIGENCE SUMMARY.
(Erase heading not required.)

XXVIII DIVISIONAL TRAIN.

Hour, Date, Place	Summary of Events and Information	Remarks and references to Appendices
WEDNESDAY 6th October 1915.	No 3 Company moves 9.30 a.m. from BETHUNE to GUARBECQUE	Ref MAP 36A P170 5:57
THURSDAY 7th "	No 4 Company moves 9.45 a.m. from BETHUNE to L'ECLEME. O.C. visits all four Companies. Vice Staff units sent to No 3 Company. One reinforcement collected by No Company + sent to 85th Fd Ambulance. Seventy nine machine guns fourteen limbered G.S. (Complete limbered) were handed over to No Company of the train by the units of 28th Division.	" MAP 36A P170 5:57 " V 3 C 55
FRIDAY 8th "	A summary of evidence taken in the case of J D'Hooge. The limbers machine guns received on 7th were issued to the II + VIII Divisions. Ninety LD + two HD horses. Remounts received from H.T. Depot 1st Army - CHOCQUES Station were distributed as follows:- No II Coy 4 HD horses 12 LD horses No III Coy 6 HD horses 8 LD horses LD Division one NCO five drivers left for THEROUANNE to take over five cobs carts - Complete animals -	
SATURDAY 9th "	LD Division returns from THEROUANNE with 5 cobs carts which were distributed as follows: One to 2 days of Leicester, one to 6.1st East Kents, one to 6.2nd H.D.R. Lancs, one to 6.1st Suffolks + one to 6th Div Gyclists. L.T. and Adjutant inspect most all refilling point. Adjutant at H.Q. Cav of Capt Robertson O.C. + Adjutant visits LT + No Coy + Australia Remounts as follows.	

Army Form C. 2118.

WAR DIARY
or
INTELLIGENCE SUMMARY.
(Erase heading not required.)

XXVIII DIVISIONAL TRAIN.   41.

Hour, Date, Place	Summary of Events and Information	Remarks and references to Appendices
SATURDAY 9th October	No II Coy. 3 HD Horses + 5 LD Horses	
	" III Coy HHD " 3 LD "	
	" IV Coy 1 HD : 12 LD "	
SUNDAY. 10th "	O.C. Adjutant to IV Company to try a case of insubordination	
	O.C. ADVS + DADMS details Pluie of 84th Brigade	
	Sgr Lieutenant G.S. Sergeant's Complete biscuits to be handed over	
	to 84th Brigade	
MONDAY. 11th "	Adjutant to proceed at 9 C. The case Driver Biggs	
	O.C. ADVS + DADMS. visits I Coy transport of 83rd Brigade	
TUESDAY. 12.	O.C. & HQrs of Division to take up duties as Claims officer	
	for 28th Division. V2 Drivers vs Transferred from III Company to HQ of Train	
	Adjutant visits HQ II + III Companies	
	Sentences of Cpl Roberton Pte Neagle promulgated - the former reduced	
WEDNESDAY. 13th	to rank of later to 1 year with hard labour	
	Six new + six Pack removals taken over at CHOCQUES Ry Station	
THURSDAY 14th	by HQ Company	
	Removals from Ball distributed as follows 2 Kettles to No II Company +	
	One Pack to No III Company one Kettle to HQ. Coy.	
FRIDAY. 15th	Lt Dobson left on five days leave	
	O.C. visits II. IV. + HQ Companies. Adjutant to 3 Coy	
	DADOS sent 1st Army despatch IV. III. + II. Companies 83rd Inf Brigade move	
	to BEUVRY	

Army Form C. 2118.

WAR DIARY
or
INTELLIGENCE SUMMARY.
(Erase heading not required.)

XXVIII DIVISIONAL TRAIN

Hour, Date, Place	Summary of Events and Information	Remarks and references to Appendices
SATURDAY Oct. 16	No 1 Company move from CONNEKAM to BETHUNE. Baggage wagons moved on 15th inst with Brigade units. Company wagons move at 8.30 am. Supply wagons (full) 9.30 am. C.O. BOETHUNE to find billets for Train H.Qrs. & the Companies.	
SUNDAY Oct 17	At 7 am Train Headquarters move from BUSNES to BETHUNE. At 9.30 am No 1 Company move from LECKEME to BETHUNE. Supply wagons move with the Company supply.	
MONDAY Oct 18	No 3 Company from GUARBECQUE to BETHUNE E.4.A.59 arriving 10.30 am. No 2 visits all Companies. Train leaves for Corbie. Offr Mem Vet-Surgeons. Cart to D.D.C. Offr to Adjutant to D.A.C. H.E. Adjutant to 1st Army Headquarters re DIVISIONAL move.	Ref: Map 36 Combined E.4.A.05
TUESDAY Oct 19	Major Rearn left Train Capt Farries acting at S.S.O. 39 A.S.C. arrives 3 Cheshire & 2 Royal Scottish all other ranks received from Horse Transport Depot ABBEVILLE.	TUESDAY, Oct 19. to PETRE to Hospital Capt Levy takes over claims officer.
WEDNESDAY 20	All Train motor cars changed for "Sunbeam" cars by Supply Column. All heavy draught horses of 3 & 8 Div 1st line exchanges for lighter ones D for meed. Three limber G.S. wagons received from 86th Field Ambulance. Motor A.S.C. drivers sent to each of the 84th 86th 86th Field Ambulances.	
THURSDAY 21st	3 Cheshire & 9 Royal Scottish transport handed over to their units. 84 Brigade & Artillery Commence to entrain Baggage wagons of the units concerned return to the Train. The following transfers take place	

[over]

Army Form C. 2118.

43

WAR DIARY
or
INTELLIGENCE SUMMARY.
(Erase heading not required.)

XXVIII DIVISIONAL TRAIN

Instructions regarding War Diaries and Intelligence Summaries are contained in F.S. Regs., Part II. and the Staff Manual respectively. Title pages will be prepared in manuscript.

Hour, Date, Place	Summary of Events and Information	Remarks and references to Appendices
THURSDAY October 21st 1915	Lt Colliard from HQ Coy to B Company, Lt Abel from HQ Coy to H Company. Lt Gallie from 3 Coy to Headquarters Officer 2 Coy, Lt Coleman to H.Q. of Coy. Lt Dixon from 3 Coy to no 2 Coy. Capt Levy from HQ Coy to 3 Coy. Lt Sayers from H Coy to HQ. Coy. Capt Rose, Capt Johnson, Lt Allans & Lt Brown with seven M.T. men. Remits to Supply details also Supply Car & two Technical Lorries complete left by rail. Transport received from 85 — 7 Ambulance — 3 limbers complete 6 mid horses. 84 — 8th Inft Brigade — 1 mdhorse, 1 rider. 2 King's own — 1 limber complete. Lt Dur Highrs — 1 Riding, 1 Pack. York & Lancs — 1 Riff limber, 3 rd horses. 85 — 7 Ambulance — 1 mdhorse. 3 musketeers — 1 Riding, 1 Pack. Infantry units received 334 other ranks. 85 Brigade in addition Enfield & SKORK rmd & Corps 10th Div.	
FRIDAY Oct 22nd 1915.	Baggage & Supply wagons. 2 following officers were appointed: Lt Solady & Quar Coleman L' Aint transport, 1 Mounts H Transport. Arrival of HQ car, no 10. 0 Rands Supply details, 7 Mounts H Transport. Limber complete turned. Received twelve complete turnouts from Royal Artillery (Baggage & Supply) 3 Baggage wagons from Cyclists Germany & Div Hqrs. Supply wagon received from SM 83rd Fd Pd Fd Ambulances.	

Army Form C. 2118.

1/4

WAR DIARY
or
INTELLIGENCE SUMMARY.
(Erase heading not required.)

XXVIII DIVISIONAL TRAIN

Instructions regarding War Diaries and Intelligence Summaries are contained in F.S. Regs., Part II. and the Staff Manual respectively. Title pages will be prepared in manuscript.

Hour, Date, Place	Summary of Events and Information	Remarks and references to Appendices
FRIDAY OCT. 22ⁿᵈ	Supply wagons from Div RE Northumbrian 50y RE, lumber from Div RA. Gen Bulfins Groom & Chargers (two). Twelve Horse four wagons & twenty two LD horses received from	
SATURDAY 23ʳᵈ	D.P.C. Arrivals. 10 baggage wagons (complete animals) received from Artillery - at limber from R.E. Headquarters. 15 Drivers RFA at limber from R.E. Headquarters. Wagons 28 LD horses to Gen RE Dawson. No. 1 & 3 Companies moved from BETHUNE to BUSNES. The following entrained Capt Bamberger with entire R.E. brilliance 11 Supply details 6 H Transport details - Army & Car - Technical retail motor Car also Lt Denny - 10 Supply details - 4 HTransport - moto Car & driver. Circles complete entrained. Chauffeurs - Cabmen etc motor Car entrained Capt Harris - Sgt Thomas. Headquarters H.Q. Company & Company moved from BETHUNE to BUSNES.	
SUNDAY 24.		
MONDAY 25.		
TUESDAY 26.	Lt visits Companies & Corps Headquarters O.C. to 1ˢᵗ Corps Headquarters - List made of myrolij who are able to do duty	
WEDNESDAY 27.	8 G.S wagons 15 killers Pr Shaw.	
THURSDAY 28.	6 G.S. rt limbered 28 horses LD Drivers RFA returned from 11 Division ⁴ᵗʰ Capt Levy left on 7 days leave - D.A.Q.M.G 1ˢᵗ Corps visited Train re Drivers received from 11 Division. H.Q. Company moved to MAP 96A 29 O 36 A8 Their details	

(73989) W4141—463. 400,000. 9/14. H.&J. Ltd. Forms/C. 2118/10.

Army Form C. 2118.

WAR DIARY
or
INTELLIGENCE SUMMARY.
(Erase heading not required.)

XXVIII DIVISIONAL TRAIN.

Hour, Date, Place	Summary of Events and Information	Remarks and references to Appendices
FRIDAY. October 29.	One G.S. wagon & 4 horses & two drivers received from 1st Brigade Guards Division. One G.S. wagon & 4 horses & two drivers received from 3rd Brigade Guards Division. N.T. mobile veterinary Sec" visited Train. 0. T. aday inspected. H.Q. no.I & no.IV Coys.	
SATURDAY 30th	Same billets	
SUNDAY 31st	Same billets	

28th Sine Jnani

Noon

Vol XI

9/C

7779

Sing

Army Form C. 2118.

WAR DIARY
or
INTELLIGENCE SUMMARY.
(Erase heading not required.)

XVIIth DIVISIONAL TRAIN

46

Hour, Date, Place	Summary of Events and Information	Remarks and references to Appendices
MONDAY NOVEMBER 1st 1915.	Lieut Dixson reported off leave. Lt Dixson posted to No. 2 Company. Measles broke out amongst EAST SURREY Infantry men.	
TUESDAY 2nd	Commanding Officer visited 1st Corps Headquarters. A party of 75 infantry men to 2nd DIVISION at ESSPIRE ESSTAIRE. A party of 29 infantry men to 7 DIVISION at BETHUNE. A similar GS & one LD horse received from Guards DIVISION. One LD horse cast for vice.	
WEDNESDAY 3	Same letters - Five men proceed on leave from H.Q. Company.	
THURSDAY 4	L⁄C. Sorrsen of Claires Connection killed with companies 6- fix up a weekly visit with farmers. Sgt ABBEY Cpl GOLDSMITH D⁄Young return off leave.	
FRIDAY 5	W.O. Ambers ½ left with 4 GS wagons (complete with team & horses) T.14 R.A Drivers for THEROUANNE. Convoy ors to proceed to P.H.T Depot ABBEVILLE. V.O. 1st ARMY Inspects horses of TRAIN.	
SATURDAY 6	Two horses LD cast to no 2 Mobile Vet Sect. 29 Infantry men - EAST SURREYS. Sent to 4th DIVISION BETHUNE. 5 men from No 2 Company left on 9 days leave. One ASC man infantry man attached reported from hospital.	
SUNDAY 7	Saw billets. # Capt LEVY returned off leave.	
MONDAY 8	Gen Dease's Charges Sent to No 2 Mobile Vet Sect for transfer to ABBEVILLE. Claims officer of BETHUNE area visits Train.	

Army Form C. 2118.

47.

WAR DIARY
or
INTELLIGENCE SUMMARY.
(Erase heading not required.)

XXVIII DIVISIONAL TRAIN

Instructions regarding War Diaries and Intelligence Summaries are contained in F. S. Regs., Part II. and the Staff Manual respectively. Title pages will be prepared in manuscript.

Hour, Date, Place	Summary of Events and Information	Remarks and references to Appendices
MONDAY NOV. 8th	7 Settlers how much to pay for rent if found occupied by Train	
TUESDAY Nov 9th	Capt Jackson No 2 Coy left on 10 days leave	
WEDNESDAY NOV 10	Same killed	
THURSDAY NOV 11th	Col Dexter DDS+T of Army visited Train & gave information that 83rd Division were coming out to this Country & that the Train would take duties with the Division.	
	Capt Walter ASC. S.S.O. 33 Division reported. also 1 Car & Chauffeur + one driver (batman)	
	Five men left on leave as follows. One from No 2 Coy from 3 Y + one from H² Coy's	
	Seven wagons meaning Shaw from ROBECQUE. No draw Drawn	
FRIDAY NOV 12.	O.C. to HQ Army AIRE. O.C. to Corps Headquarters CHOCQUE.	
SATURDAY. NOV 13.	Four Supply Officers Capts. NORCOCK. BARRY CRUICKSHANK. POPE with four Supply Cars four drivers four batmen reported 8.30 am & posted with HQ Coy. No 2. 3. + 4 Coys respectively.	
	Refilling Point BUSNES. 8.30 am for all Companies	
	Train moves from BUSNES at 9 am to following places.	

Army Form C. 2118
48

WAR DIARY
or
INTELLIGENCE SUMMARY.
(Erase heading not required.)

XVIIIth DIVISIONAL TRAIN

Instructions regarding War Diaries and Intelligence Summaries are contained in F.S. Regs., Part II. and the Staff Manual respectively. Title pages will be prepared in manuscript.

Hour, Date, Place	Summary of Events and Information	Remarks and references to Appendices
SATURDAY. NOVEMBER 13.	Headquarters of Train to MORBECQUES. Village. H.Q. Company to MORBECQUES No 2. Company to THIENNES. No 3. Company to STIENBECQUES. No 4. Company to BOSENGHEM. O.C. + S.O. to Army Headquarters	
SUNDAY. No. 14.	O.C. + S.O. look for refilling points & located at MAP. 26A. C 28.D. for 98 Brigade C 28.B. 9.0. 99 Brigade C 29 C.D. for 100 Brigade C 24.B. for D.V. Troops. O.C. to 1st Army Headquarters with adjutant. DAA + QMG 33 Division arrives	
MONDAY. Nov. 15.	O.C. to 1st Army Headquarters. Oraelle room at 3 Company. to HQ Coy. 7 refilling points - 98th Brigade Supply wagons located.	
TUESDAY. Nov. 16.	Lt Squirl undertake lost for billets for QMaster at BLENDEQUE. O.C. visits refilling points & Railhead for detraining – 98 Brigade + H.Q. Division arrive. Some men return letter off leave Twenty Seven Drivers arrive from ABBEVILLE.	
WEDNESDAY. Nov. 17.	The following officers arrived Capt. Illingworth N.S. Casswell P. Coventry J. Myers D. Q'ment Boys M.A. also 4 Riders - 4 Sergts	

www.ingramcontent.com/pod-product-compliance
Lightning Source LLC
Chambersburg PA
CBHW081241170426
43191CB00034B/2008